Alternatives

Games,

exercises and

conversations

for the

language

classroom

Pilgrims

**Richard and
Marjorie Baudains**

Longman

Longman Group UK Limited,
Longman House, Burnt Mill, Harlow,
Essex CM20 2JE, England
and Associated Companies throughout the world.

© Longman Group UK Limited 1990

This book is produced in association
with Pilgrims Language Courses Limited
of Canterbury, England.

First published 1990
Third impression 1991

Set in Linotron 10/12pt Cheltenham

Printed in Great Britain
by Richard Clay plc, Bungay, Suffolk

British Library Cataloguing in Publication Data
Baudains, Richard
    Alternatives: games, exercises and conversations for
    the language classroom.
    (Pilgrims Longman teachers resource books)
    1. Non-English speaking students.
    Curriculum subjects: English language. Teaching
    I. Title   II. Baudains, Marjorie   III. Series
    428.2407

ISBN 0582 03767 0

Illustrations
Cover illustrated by Peter Tucker

A letter from the Series Editors

Dear Teacher,

This series of teachers' resource books has developed from Pilgrims' involvement in running courses for learners of English and for teachers and teacher trainers.

Our aim is to pass on ideas, techniques and practical activities which we know work in the classroom. Our authors, both Pilgrims teachers and like-minded colleagues in other organisations, present accounts of innovative procedures which will broaden the range of options available to teachers working within communicative and humanistic approaches.

We would be very interested to receive your impressions of the series. If you notice any omissions that we ought to rectify in future editions, or if you think of any interesting variations, please let us know. We will be glad to acknowledge all contributions that we are able to use.

Seth Lindstromberg   *Mario Rinvolucri*
Series Editor   Series Consultant

Pilgrims Language Courses
Canterbury
Kent
CT1 3HG
England

Richard and Marjorie Baudains

Richard and Marjorie Baudains came into TEFL in 1976 and have been involved in teacher-training since the early 1980s. They have worked as trainers, together and separately, in Britain, Italy, China and Poland for Pilgrims and the British Council.

Richard has an MA in TESOL from University of London's Institute of Education and is currently Group Director of Studies for the British Schools of Friuli-Venezia Giulia in Italy. He has written materials for language teaching for both English and Italian. His special interests are staff development, TEFL methodology and working with groups.

Marjorie is a former Director of Studies at Pilgrims, whose special interests include the visual arts in language teaching, Community Language Learning and unorthodox methodologies. Her current occupation is that of mother and housewife. Together with Richard she contributes regularly to the magazine *Practical English Teaching*.

Acknowledgements

This book is dedicated to Sandra and Mario.

Contents

Index of activities

Introduction

THE AIM OF THIS BOOK

All round the world students sit in class and do exercises which many of them, regardless of their age, level or reason for studying English, find frankly and unequivocally boring, but which somebody somewhere (not necessarily the teacher – it could be a ministry of education, a text book writer, a headteacher) considers are necessary. Teachers respond to this situation in different ways. Some become resigned to what they see as the basic truth that learning a foreign language naturally entails doing work of the 'boring but necessary' type. Others spend their careers trying to find more interesting ways to teach the parts of their syllabus and materials that they know from experience their students find tedious and demotivating.

It's not easy to sustain the argument that learners should always find immediate enjoyment in their class work, and even more difficult to support it with practical ideas that will stimulate students and educators in an infinity of different teaching situations. Nevertheless this is what the present book aims to do, by describing sixty classroom techniques and suggesting, in this introduction, a way of categorising TEFL activity types which gives a criterion for devising lessons that motivate.

THE ISSUE OF MOTIVATION

The way students respond to the activities we ask them to do is one of the cruxes of successful learning. As far as we can ever say we see learning taking place, most teachers would guess we observe it in the state of total engagement in an activity in which students are busy but relaxed, feeling positive emotions as they work and become absorbed in the task in hand to the point where they are often unaware of the passing of time. On the other hand, it is difficult to believe that bored, alienated students plodding distractedly through exercises despite their own inclinations are achieving anything significant. Some learners may be stimulated by a long term aim (job, travel, exams) to apply themselves to kinds of study which are uncongenial to them, but in many EFL situations, to be realistic, this is not a motivation teachers can depend on. What counts for all kinds of learners, however, is the way they feel about whatever they do in class, at the moment in which they do it. To put it simply, some activities are motivating and others are not.

A WAY OF CATEGORISING TEFL ACTIVITIES

Any systematic attempt to identify what any one group of learners finds stimulating needs to categorise classroom activities. Our current, eclectic TEFL culture has sophisticated ways of doing this on the basis of linguistic, dynamic and pedagogic features. When we talk about activities we are familiar with distinctions between, for example:

fluency – accuracy
practice – production
language based – skills based
micro skill – macro skill ⎫ activities
active – passive
authentic – simulated
controlled – open ended

Important as these distinctions may be from the teacher's perspective, it's unlikely that they are part of the learner's mental frame, or that they make much difference to the way students feel about activities. What I have tried to do in this book is to categorise the things teachers get students to do from the students' point of view. It seems to me that learners, on a purely intuitive basis, perceive a very limited number of activity types and distinguish between them according to what they see as their immediate purpose. Independent of method or approach, I believe that people who study English are motivated by one or more of four possible reasons for doing an activity in class; having fun, studying language, sharing real information and showing what they know (or don't know). These purposes correspond to the students' activity types. The first three are teaching activities: *Games*, *Exercises* and *Conversations*. The fourth category is that of evaluation, or *Tests*. These categories are shown in Fig. 1.

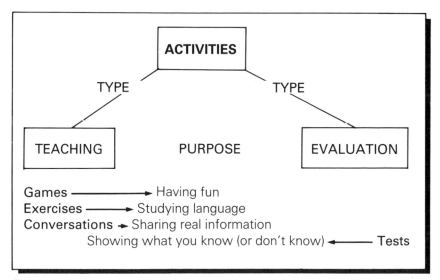

Fig. 1

The three teaching activities are the subject of this book. The idea of the test as a students' category is discussed here in the introduction, although evaluation procedures are outside the scope of the main part of the book, because tests generally have an important place in students' perceptions of school work and an important effect on motivation.

A WAY OF DEFINING TEFL ACTIVITY TYPES

The meanings of the words used to describe activity types need explanation since I have broadened their usual definitions. In this context, Activity is the umbrella term for all kinds of structured student behaviour, introduced by the teacher with the general aim of furthering mastery of the foreign language. Conversation, Exercise, Game and Test denote types of activity. They all have the aim of 'furthering mastery of the foreign language' that students will be more or less aware of as they do them. They also have immediate objectives that students cannot help being conscious of and which, while they contribute to the general aim, may be different from it. For instance, when students are absorbed in a discussion in the foreign language they are working towards the aim of improving oral skills, but their immediate objective is to exchange opinions. Involvement in the immediate objective is the motivating factor which, I argue, brings an activity to life and makes it meaningful to a student. It is on the basis of the learners' reason for doing the work the teacher proposes – what could be called the authentic purpose of an activity – that I distinguish between Games, Exercises, Conversations and Tests.

THE CATEGORIES
Games

Games are activities students do for their own sake, for the immediate fun, curiosity or competitive ambition aroused by the Game. This category includes conventional puzzles and competitions, but also all activities involving make-believe such as drama and story telling which people do for fun. Poetry writing can be a Game (playing with words) or a Conversation (expressing opinions and feelings).

Exercises

These activities have the explicit objective of learning or practising the forms, sounds and meanings of English. This kind of work has always been the bedrock of foreign language study, often consisting of mechanical repetition, transformation or memorisation, the epitome of all that is 'boring but necessary'. Focusing explicitly on language as content need not be intrinsically demotivating, however. Practice for practice's sake, when it involves new understanding, can be effective and rewarding learning. The criteria of a stimulating Exercise are probably the elements of intellectual challenge and discovery – working things out for yourself, for example, in the ways devised by Gattegno in his Silent Way – although not all learners are motivated by these factors and not all activities perceived as Exercises are intended as such. This last point is developed further on.

Conversations

The reason for doing this kind of activity is to exchange facts, opinions, experiences and feelings which are important for the interlocutors. The key is the authenticity of the content and the desire to communicate. Students talk to each other and to the teacher about real things. The discussion lesson is the most obvious example, but highly motivating structured Conversations can be devised with grammatical aims, without losing the authentic purpose of communication.

Tests

These are activities which students perceive as exposing them to the judgement of either the teacher or their peers, and go beyond the formal test to include also anything which the learner feels is covertly evaluative. Reading aloud answers from a written exercise is a Test for most people. Tests are clearly important, but generally have an element of threat.

SOME ASSUMPTIONS ABOUT THE CATEGORIES

The activities in this book are divided into three sections: Games, Exercises and Conversations. One of the assumptions is that the effectiveness of an activity is relative to students' response to it and that no one type of activity is in itself more motivating than any other. What some groups will find engaging will perhaps alienate others in different situations. Pupils doing compulsory English in the first years of secondary school rarely find Exercises motivating, although some might want to do well in tests and apply themselves accordingly, but find genuine enjoyment in Games and Conversations. On the other hand, adults who study English for their work are often attracted to Exercises because they associate them with serious, purposeful learning and want Tests to give them frequent evidence of their progress. These are generalisations for the purpose of illustration and certainly not hard and fast rules. The same point could be made by citing groups of adults and secondary school learners who have the opposite responses.

Another important premise is that, inevitably, the grouping of the activities in this book is based on a teacher's (my own) view of their potential purpose for learners. What for one group is a Game, however, may be an Exercise for another. The categorisation is subjective. Many activities in class are received as Exercises by default because the students have missed the authentic purpose the teacher had in mind. If students don't enter into the make-believe of a role play, accept the challenge of a competition or have their curiosity awakened by a puzzle, all these Game activities become mere language practice. Conversely, learners often do multiple-choice activities, which are conceived as Tests or Exercises by their authors, in the spirit of a Game, engaged by the puzzle or game of chance element.

Cross-perception of the purpose of an activity by teacher and students is very common. Once, in the first lesson with a new group, I asked some students to make a list of questions they would like to ask each other. One wrote: *Can Arthur dance? You are Italian, aren't you?* Arthur was the fictitious hero of the course book. The class were all Italians. The students had interpreted the purpose of the activity as that of (meaningless) language practice, while what I had intended was for students to do a short Conversation (real questions about things which interested them).

A frequent cross-perception is Conversation – Test, where the teacher expects the group to discuss spontaneously but the students fail to respond because, self-conscious about making errors, they perceive the activity as a risk loaded Test.

USES OF THE CATEGORIES

I have found the idea of the four basic activity types useful in a number of ways. It has given me a new perspective on balance – the balance of activity types – in my own teaching and in the observation of colleagues and trainees. In my experience, students' responses to activity types arc more important for motivation than topic, and I've been able to activate 'difficult' groups by emphasising their preferred mode. In this connection, an area for continuing experiment is the challenge of finding different ways to work at the same skills and language points; what could be respectively a Game, Conversation and Exercise approach to teaching the second conditional, developing commercial letter-writing skills or improving intensive listening? This seems to me an important question because it's one that can help liberate teachers and learners from the tyranny of the 'boring but necessary'.

This selection of activities has been inspired by several special teachers who work in different fields in radically different ways, by various and sometimes contrasting approaches to TEFL and by fringe disciplines such as drama and in-service training. Teachers and learners evolve their own approaches from sources like these. We hope that this book, besides providing successful lessons, will suggest new ways to adapt teaching materials and put syllabuses into practice.

MORE ABOUT THIS BOOK

The activities in this book are intended to supplement or transform basic course material. Sometimes the book will show you, the teacher, a way to work with a story, a song, a vocabulary list or a structure which you select. Other times it focuses on universal themes such as the family, personal description or the home.

In the preliminaries for each activity we describe its objectives and suggest the appropriate level(s) but not the age or type of learner. We have aimed for a collection that will be relevant to as wide a range of users as possible, from junior secondary school to adults. We give an idea of the time you will need for the activity and the materials. The notes at the end contain ideas for follow-ups, variations or sources where this seems useful.

Richard Baudains
Greve in Chianti
January 1989

CHAPTER 1

Games

THINGS THAT ARE RED

A vocabulary and question practice game based on the fascination of inventing lists.

Procedure

1 Ask the students to work individually to each make a list of ten things that are red, which they must not show to anyone.
2 Wait until everyone has finished and then get students into pairs, sitting face to face.
3 Explain that the aim of the game is to see who in each pair can guess the most things from their partner's list in three minutes by asking *Yes/No* questions. (They must start with the first item on the list and work down one by one). If the game is not clear, give a quick demonstration with a student. A typical exchange might go like this:
   Item number one, is it big?
   No.
   Is it a fruit?
   Yes.
   Does it grow on trees?
   No.
   Is it a strawberry?
   Yes.
4 Ask the students to decide who will begin in each group and then give the signal to start. Stop after three minutes and change roles. At the end of the second period of questions, count the scores. If the students are seriously involved in the competitive element, it's important to be scrupulously fair about the timing.

NOTES

Loren McGrail taught us the idea of having students group words under big, universal headings.

VARIATIONS

Other possible lists include things that are: fragile, blue, dangerous, dirty, noisy, hot.

1.1

LANGUAGE FOCUS
Vocabulary expansion; question forms, oral practice

LEVEL
Elementary +

TIME
10–15 minutes

MATERIALS
Pen and paper

PREPARATION
None

1.2

LANGUAGE FOCUS
Revision of past
participles

LEVEL
Lower intermediate

TIME
10 minutes

MATERIALS
One set of grammar
pelmanism cards for
every four to five
students

GRAMMAR PELMANISM

An example of how card games can be adapted for language teaching.

PREPARATION

Make a list of the verbs and their past participles that you want the class to revise. You need at least fifteen verbs for the game to be interesting. Take a supply of plain white cards (for fifteen verbs you will need thirty cards) which must be all the same size. Write the infinitives and the past participles of your verbs on the cards, one word per card. This makes a set. Duplicate for each group of four to five students.

Procedure

1 Divide the class into groups, each group sitting around a table, and hand out the cards.
2 The students spread the cards on the table face down and then take turns at picking up two cards at a time. The object is to find the past participle and the infinitive of the same verb. If a student picks up a matching pair they keep it. If the two cards don't go together they must be replaced face down in the same place as they came from. The group adjudicates disputes about what makes a pair. Continue until all the cards have been picked up. The winner is the player with the most cards at the end.

NOTES

This kind of activity is ideal for individualised class work in which sub-groups tackle different tasks according to their needs and interests.

1.3

LANGUAGE FOCUS
Oral practice

LEVEL
Intermediate +

TIME
15–20 minutes

MATERIALS
The board and a die
for every four players
(but see Notes
below)

A BOARD GAME

A lateral thinking game which generates discussion by asking the players to decide the scoring by concensus.

PREPARATION

Take a piece of card approximately 30 cm × 30 cm and divide it into thirty-six squares. Number the squares in sequence. Collect ten to twelve pictures of everyday objects from magazine illustrations and stick them on random squares around the board (see Fig. 2).

Procedure

1 The game is played in groups of four. Each player needs a coin to use as a counter. Everybody starts from square one.
2 The first player throws the die and moves the number of squares indicated. If the counter lands on a picture, the player must propose three possible uses for the object depicted.

3 The group must then decide (majority decision) whether or not the answer is acceptable, rejecting any ideas they think are impossible. The player who has made the proposals can argue in favour of them, but cannot add any new ones. If the group accepts the answer, the player moves forward two squares, otherwise they must go back two. The first player to arrive at the last square is the winner.

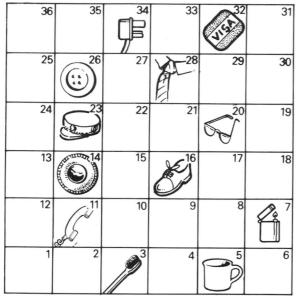

Fig. 2

NOTES

If you want the whole class to play the game at the same time you will obviously need to make a number of boards. Alternatively you can use the board game as one of a number of different activities in an individualised classwork session. The British Council film *Communication Games* (1978) shows this kind of classroom management in action. Other board games for language learning appear in *Grammar Games* (Rinvolucri 1984).

1.4

LANGUAGE FOCUS
Numbers, listening

LEVEL
Beginner

TIME
5 minutes

MATERIALS
Black/whiteboard
and pens or chalk of
two different colours

PREPARATION
None

NUMBERS GRAB

A listening activity to help train discrimination and speed up responses, which is useful for beginners who lack confidence in their own listening comprehension. Although only two players take part at a time, the whole class is involved in the same mental effort as the students in the game.

Procedure

1 Write a selection of about fifteen numbers the class have learned in a random scatter pattern on the board. Include any which cause difficulty either singly or in contrast (e.g. '13' and '30').
2 Have two students come to the board and stand facing it with a pen or chalk of a different colour at the ready.
3 Call out the numbers on the board one by one. As they hear them, the students race each other to make a circle around the number you have called (each number can only be ringed once). At the end, the student who has ringed the most numbers is the winner.
4 Repeat the game with new players and different numbers. Have students from the class call out the numbers.

VARIATIONS

This game can be used for any list of new vocabulary. To make the listening task more sophisticated, use all minimal pairs.

1.5

LANGUAGE FOCUS
Adjectives

LEVEL
Lower
intermediate +

TIME
10 minutes

MATERIALS
Magazine adverts

DUNCAN'S ADJECTIVES GAME

A speed reading and cloze test competition using magazine advertisements, a perfect authentic source for work on adjectives.

PREPARATION

Choose seven or eight magazine adverts with big print and not too much text and number them clearly. Black out two adjectives from each advert and make a list of the missing words. Before the lesson, post the adverts on the walls, spacing them out around the classroom.

Procedure

1 Dictate the list of adjectives and tell the students that these are the words which have been cancelled from the adverts around the walls.
2 Explain the competition. The object is to find the advert to which each word on the students' list belongs in the shortest possible time. The students race from text to text, in any order, noting for each adjective the number of the advert from which they think it comes. The winner is either the first to finish or the one with the most correct solutions after five minutes.

3 At the end of the game, check the answers with the class, being careful not to leave out acceptable alternatives to the original texts.

NOTES

This is a party game invented by Duncan Gibson.

THE STORY QUIZ

A puzzle activity for group discussion which leads to writing.

PREPARATION

1 Choose a story or anecdote of 500–1,000 words which you think the class will find challenging. It might be a text from your syllabus.
2 Prepare seven comprehension questions on the text, of the type often used to check if learners have understood the gist of a story.
3 Write each question on a separate piece of white card, about 8 cm × 13 cm. Do not number the questions. This makes one set. You will need duplicate sets for each group of four people in the class.

Procedure

1 Divide the class into groups and sit them side by side at tables (if they sit around the table some people will have to read upside down).
2 Explain that you are going to hand out a series of questions. When the answers to these questions are put together they will make a story. Students have complete freedom to arrange the sequence of the questions and answer them as they think best. Each group will have a different story from the same questions.
3 Hand out the cards.
4 Tell the students to decide the sequence in which they want to tackle the questions and put them face up on the table in this order. Check everybody has understood this step.
5 Ask them to discuss the answers, beginning with the first card. When the group has agreed on this answer, they turn over the card and write it on the back. This card now stays on the table with the answer showing and the group goes on to the next question. The activity continues in this way with the students turning over one card at a time, until all the questions have been answered.
6 At the end ask the students to tell (not read) their stories to each other. You can do this as a whole class activity, or re-form the groups so that each member comes from a different team and has a different story to tell.

NOTES

This is an adaptation of a game devised by J-P. Créton. *Once Upon a Time* (Morgan and Rinvolucri 1984) is about using stories in TEFL.

1.6

LANGUAGE FOCUS
Oral practice, writing

LEVEL
Intermediate +

TIME
30–40 minutes

MATERIALS
One set of quiz cards (see below) for each group of four students

1.7

LANGUAGE FOCUS
Vocabulary
expansion

LEVEL
Elementary –
intermediate

TIME
15 minutes

MATERIALS
Pen and paper; a
short narrative text

LIGHTNING SKETCHES

This is a vocabulary search activity which helps students get imaginatively involved in preparing for the reading of a narrative text.

PREPARATION

Choose a text, which could be an extract from a longer work, that describes events that take place in a single setting. The location should be clear from the opening sentence. Here is an example from *Three Singles to Adventure* by Gerald Durrell (Penguin 1965):

In a tiny bar in the back streets of Georgetown four of us sat around a table, sipping rum and ginger beer and pondering a problem.

Procedure

1 The students should be ready with pen in hand and a blank piece of paper in front of them.
2 Explain that you are going to read the beginning of a story. The students must imagine themselves entering the place where this story is set, looking around, observing the details of the scene.
3 As soon as you stop reading, the students should fill their page with lightning sketches of the objects they saw in their image of the place where the story is set. They are not drawing the whole scene, but collecting random images of things contained in it. There is a time limit of three minutes. The aim is to work as fast as possible and not to worry about the artistic quality of the sketches.
4 At the end of three minutes get the students into pairs and have them exchange papers.
5 Ask them to label the objects they see on the page in front of them, without discussing the task with their partner (stress this rule).
6 When they have finished, partners sit side by side and check the outcome of the labelling. This will involve identifying obscure drawings and finding new English words. Circulate and provide vocabulary as needed.
7 Go ahead with the reading of the text when this activity is finished.

NOTES

This is a variation on an idea published in *Vocabulary* (Morgan and Rinvolucri 1986).

THE INANIMATE NARRATOR

A technique for re-telling stories which allows for creative interpretation and dialogue between narrator and audience.

PREPARATION

Choose a text for each group (it could be a picture story) and make copies for all the group members.

Procedure

1 Arrange the students in groups of three or four, sitting in a tight circle.
2 Hand out the texts and allow time for reading and discussion in the groups of any comprehension difficulties. Make sure everyone is happy that they have understood the story.
3 Now ask each student to choose a different inanimate object which features in their story and which interests them, then ask them to read the text again and imagine how the story would be told if it were written by the object they have chosen.
4 Change the seating so that, while still in groups, the students can see all the other class members.
5 Ask each group to tell its story to the class, each member speaking in turn and narrating the events from the point of view of the object of their choice, in the first person. Remind them that each object can only describe what they can reasonably know about, and that the inanimate narrators may have different information about the people and the story. The audience asks questions to clarify and expand as they listen.

NOTES

The game is fun because it's improvised. If you allow lots of time to prepare, the re-telling of the activity loses momentum. The strong element of collective make-believe makes possible for a group what might be embarrassingly silly for a single student.

This activity can also be used to introduce texts from the syllabus. In this case all the students have the same text and individuals volunteer to be questioned by the group in the role of different objects. One class were able to discover important details about the lives of the characters in Laurie Lee's *Cider with Rosie* by interviewing the clock on the wall from a passage describing the family kitchen.

1.8

LANGUAGE FOCUS
Oral practice

LEVEL
Lower
intermediate +

TIME
20–30 minutes

MATERIALS
A short narrative text
for each group of
three or four
students

1.9

LANGUAGE FOCUS
Describing sounds

LEVEL
Upper-intermediate
–advanced

TIME
20–30 minutes

MATERIALS
Pen and paper, a
copy of the text for
each student

THE SOUNDS OF THE TEXT

A vocabulary search linked to a reading which gives another unusual entry route to the text. The technique can bring interest to less-than-inspiring EFL course material.

PREPARATION

Choose a text from your course book, or another source. It could be something suggested by the class. The activity is possible with most types of writing, including poems, songs, narrative, newspaper articles and even discursive texts, although very abstract ones are less suitable.

Procedure

1 Ask the class to get comfortable, relax and be perfectly silent for one minute. During this time they should close their eyes and focus all their attention on their sense of hearing. Ask them to concentrate on picking out all the sounds around them, and then, at the end of a minute, write down everything they heard.

2 Compare the results together and then try to categorise the sounds under different headings. Sounds can be, for example, human or mechanical, distant or near, loud or soft, single or repetitive, pleasant or jarring.

   Without overburdening the students with vocabulary, work on some of the lexical possibilities for describing sound in English (verbs for instance: *hum, whirr, buzz, scrape, scuffle, scratch, shuffle*, etc.).

3 Now hand out the texts and put the students into groups of three or four. Ask them to go through the reading and, working together in the group, list all the sounds the text contains or suggests.

4 At the end of the task the groups report back, compare different lists and share insights.

NOTES

The first part of the activity is an idea from *Drama Techniques in Language Learning* New Edition (Maley and Duff 1982).

VARIATIONS

An interesting variation is to comb a text for the colours it contains or suggests.

TEAM JIGSAWS

An activity which asks the students to solve a group management problem. One of the objectives of the game is for the learners to discover through experience the value of group cooperation. There is no explicit instruction in the rules to work as a team, and in our experience the first instinct of many students is to try to solve the problem individually, or even in competition with the others around the table.

From the language skills point of view, the activity aims at developing reading memory.

PREPARATION

1 Choose a story which can be told in ten or twelve sentences. Write it out on A4 paper, beginning each sentence at the left hand margin and leaving a space between them, then cut the page into strips so you have one sentence on each strip. Duplicate the material for each group of four or five students.
2 Before the class, write the rules of the game on the board so the learners can refer to them as they go along.

Rules

- Each person can only pick up one piece of paper at a time.
- As soon as you have read the paper you must put it back on the table, face down.
- You cannot show the piece of paper to anyone.
- The time limit for the game is seven minutes.
- As soon as you have found the story, raise your hand.

Procedure

1 In class, divide the students into groups, each sitting each around their own table.
2 Explain the task. You are going to lay face down on the tables a number of pieces of paper. Each slip has a sentence on it. When the sentences are put together in the right order they make a story. The task is to find the story, following the rules of the game.
3 Put the jigsaw stories on the tables, start timing seven minutes and check that everybody is following the rules.
4 It's very unlikely that anyone will finish inside seven minutes. Stop the activity at the end of the time limit and have students review what they have done so far. It's also very unlikely that the group will have discussed a strategy for the task. Ask them to spend a few minutes making a plan and then to start looking for the story again.
5 The first group to finish *tells* the story (NB the story cannot be read because the papers are still face down).
6 At the end of the game, ask the students to draw some conclusions about the way they tackled the problem.

1.10

LANGUAGE FOCUS
Reading; oral practice

LEVEL
Intermediate

TIME
15–20 minutes

MATERIALS
A jigsaw story (see below) for each group of four or five students

NOTES

Challenge to Think (Frank, Rinvolucri and Berer 1982) collects a number of jigsaw stories, ready to use, and suggests a different method of exploiting them.

1.11

LANGUAGE FOCUS
Vocabulary revision and expansion, oral practice

LEVEL
Elementary +

TIME
15 minutes

MATERIALS
Fifteen to twenty lengths of different coloured ribbon and/ or string

PREPARATION
None

RIBBONS

A vocabulary search activity based on the collective imagination of the class.

Procedure

1 Seat the students in a circle.
2 Give the ribbons, rolled loosely into a ball, to a volunteer, who comes to the centre of the ring and throws them gently into the air.
3 The activity consists in finding pictures in the pattern of scattered ribbons. Nominate a secretary whose job it is to list all the objects the class perceive. Try to keep away from arguments of the type: *It's a camel! No it isn't, it's a weasel!* Ask students to explain what they see and accept the natural range of interpretation.
4 Have the secretary read back the list of vocabulary, then repeat the game.

NOTES

This activity was suggested by the primary school work of Sandra Devigili. Sandra also uses paper dots made by hole punching machines to create random patterns for interpretation.

In this kind of vocabulary work in TEFL it's useful for the students to know questions such as: *What's the English word for . . .?*, *What do you call the thing which . . .?*, etc.

FREE VERSE

An activity which helps students create a 'found' poem. It's important, however, not to explain the aim of the lesson or to introduce the activity with any remarks about writing verse. The exaggerated prestige attached to poetry by school curricula makes most people feel inadequate to the task of composing it. If they know the finished product is supposed to be a poem, students censor their work so heavily that they rarely get beyond the opening lines, and suffer considerable frustration and sense of failure as a consequence. The excitement and sense of achievement in this game comes from the students' discovery of poetry in their own writing.

PREPARATION

Make ten questions appropriate to the level of your group which will elicit statements about physical and emotional sensations. Try to find questions which students may not have considered before and which will challenge their imagination and powers of expression. Here is a set of questions we have used with advanced students:

What is the sound you hear when you are inside a car and it's raining heavily outside?
What is the taste of lemons?
How do you feel when you wake up and you know it's Sunday?
What does hair feel like?
What is the sound you make walking through fresh snow?
How do you feel if you hear someone shouting your name very loud?
How can you describe the sensation of putting your hand in ice-cold water?
How do you feel when you walk in through the doors of a hospital?
What is the happiest sound in the world?
What does spring smell like?

The questions should be in random order. Don't try to find a thematic sequence.

Procedure

1 If you think it's necessary, do a short concentration exercise before beginning (see Notes, p. 18).
2 Explain to the students that you are going to ask a number of questions to which they must give written answers. The activity has a number of special features and they must pay attention to the following instructions:
   - The answers need not be written in complete sentences. An answer can be in note form; a short phrase or a single word.
   - If anyone is unable to think of an answer, don't worry, write nothing and wait for the next question, but don't leave a space.
   - Begin a new piece of paper for this activity.
   - Start writing on the third line from the top.

1.12

LANGUAGE FOCUS
Listening comprehension; writing

LEVEL
Intermediate +

TIME
30–40 minutes

MATERIALS
Pre-prepared set of questions (for the teacher only), pen and paper

- Write each answer on a separate line, starting from the left hand margin.
  Do not number the answers.

3 Read out the questions one by one, allowing time for the students to write but without waiting too long. People should be writing spontaneously, and not pondering the answers at length.

4 At the end of the question session, ask the students to study what they have written and work out the best way to read it aloud, from beginning to end.

5 Invite a couple of students to read out their work and ask the class to notice how words and phrases can be either linked or separated to create rhythmic patterns and units of meaning. Then go on to the next phase.

6 Tell the students they can expand their texts to make a piece of free verse by following this procedure:
- They can put a new word or words after the last one they have written on each line.
- They can lengthen the lines they want in this way, but they cannot insert new language in any other places in the text.
- They cannot change existing words.
- They cannot take anything away.

7 When they have done this, ask the students to give their verses a title which they should write at the top of the page.

8 One way to pool the completed work is to place an empty chair at the front of the class and invite students who want to share their writing to take the seat and read it out to the class (a powerful experience for smaller groups). If you choose this option, it's a good idea to sit among the students. Another possibility is to post the work on the walls and allow the class five to ten minutes to circulate and read it, then return to their seats and comment (more practical for large groups).
Here is an example of what students can achieve.

Drops on the window suddenly wake me from my dream
Soft, wonderful dreams interrupted by a shout;
Somebody wants me to listen or to help, I thought.
Good refreshing experiences but
I have to force myself to walk on.
Words after silence
Rain in the air
I enjoy turning round once more
Both nice and sour, night and day.

7th July 1989

NOTES

The activity needs a reasonable degree of alertness and serious concentration on the part of the students. If the group is not in this state of mind, use a short activity to help them focus on the lesson. Here is a simple technique:

Tell the class you are going to ask them to do something which needs all their attention. To help them prepare, you are going to count very slowly from one to ten. As they hear the numbers pass, they will gradually clear their minds of distractions until, when they hear the number ten, they are relaxed, alert and ready to start.

Gamester's Handbook (Brandes 1982, 1987) is a good source to consult for concentration activities.

MIXED LANGUAGE LISTENING

This is an approach to extensive listening for monolingual classes which can help learners at any level improve their ability to follow long stretches of spoken English. It has two main features. Firstly there is no pressure on the students to complete a task, and hence no element of test. The aim is to create, through the foreign language, a few minutes of pleasurable day-dreaming for the class. The second feature is the use of two languages. By combining L1 and the foreign language it's possible to write a text at any level which will give students access to ideas that would be otherwise inaccessible in a passage entirely in the target language.

The proportion of L1 to the foreign language depends on the level of the group. We have used the technique with beginners (words and phrases of the target language embedded in L1) and with intermediate students (obscure words and phrases spoken in L1 in the stream of a text prepared in the foreign language).

PREPARATION

Work out a monologue similar to the one in the example below. It should take two or three minutes to relate – about the same time as a pop music 'single'.

Procedure

1 Ask the class to put away books, pens, papers and other encumbrances, get into a comfortable position, relax and listen to your voice. Slowly recount the fantasy to the class, quietly and smoothly. Here is an example of a passage, for post elementary groups.

The teacher's voice *ronza*. The other students have their heads down over their books. You look around then slowly get up and walk in *punta di piedi* to the door. Open it. Leave the room. Now you are walking down the corridor, towards another door which is *socchiusa*. Push it open. You *rimani senza fiato*! In front of you is a vast sandy

---

1.13

LANGUAGE FOCUS
Extensive listening

LEVEL
Beginner +

TIME
10–15 minutes

MATERIALS
A mixed language text

desert. *Battendo gli occhi* you begin to walk. The hot sand *pizzica* the soles of your feet.

Soon you come to a nomad tent made of *pelle*. It smells *forte*. The door of the tent *sbatte al vento*. You *rannicchiarti* and go in.

Inside it's much bigger than you imagined. In the centre of the floor a fire burns with a *fumo dolciastro*. On the right there is a low ebony table. Move your hand along its surface, hard and *liscia*. On the table you see a *pugnale* and a *melograno*, and a *vasoio* full of rose petals, with the scents of a thousand gardens.

On the opposite side there is a heavy velvet *tenda* with exotic *ricami*. *Spingerti avanti* and see, on the floor, a *scrigno* made of ivory. As you move towards it you hear voices. Turn, go past the *tenda*, leave the *fumo dolciastro*, the *pugnale*, the *melograno*, the rose petals and return to the desert. The sand is cool now. It's after *tramonto*. Hurry to the door, open it, walk down the corridor and find your classroom again. Go *furtivamente* back to your place. Nobody *si accorge*. The teacher's voice still *ronza*.

2 At the end of the day-dream allow the students a few moments to bring their attention back to the classroom, then invite comments, but don't call on students to speak. The activity should conclude with an open, free-wheeling exchange of questions and impressions. If you are working with a beginner or elementary class, you might want to have the students talk about the day-dream in their first language.

NOTES

The idea of mixed language texts comes from *Vocabulary* (Morgan and Rinvolucri 1986). *Caring and sharing in the foreign language classroom* (Moskowitz 1978) has a section on using fantasies in TEFL.

1.14

LANGUAGE FOCUS
Listening

LEVEL
Elementary +

TIME
5 minutes

MATERIALS
None

PREPARATION
None

ROLE PLAY HANDSHAKES

This is an ice-breaking game. Ice-breakers need not be confined to the first meeting of a group. There will always be moments when the students are tense, sleepy, grumpy, bored or otherwise unready to do their best work. Activities like this one can inject energy and bring the group together.

Procedure

1 Have the students leave their places and come to a space where they can move around.
2 Ask them to walk round the space, trying not to bump into each other. When you see the students moving reasonably unselfconsciously, give the following instructions:

a Stop!
b Look at the person nearest you. You've just played the last point of the final at Wimbledon. One of you is the new champion. Don't say anything, just shake hands.
c Then move around again.
3 Repeat this process, keeping the pace brisk, until all or at least most of the students have shaken hands together.

VARIATIONS

The situations you give the students will depend on the level. Here are some suggestions for an intermediate class:

You are world leaders. You have just signed a unilateral disarmament treaty.
You're the boss and a new employee. It's the first morning of your first job.
You are the winner of £500,000 on the football pools, receiving your cheque.
You are a patient leaving hospital, shaking hands with the doctor who has just put your right arm in plaster.
You are two prime ministers at a summit. One of you is a woman.
You are two businessmen who have just completed a deal. Each thinks he's swindling the other.
You are life-long friends shaking hands through prison bars.
You are an animal trainer and a tiger in a circus.
You are a priest and a widow after a funeral.
You are two school children forced to make peace by your teacher after a fight.
You're a politician canvassing in the street.

CANS OF COCA-COLA

An inter-group competition in lateral thinking which can lead to project work.

Procedure

1 Divide the class into teams of ten to fifteen.
2 Send the teams to different corners of the room where you have previously hung the poster paper on the wall.
3 Get each group to nominate a secretary, who takes a felt tip pen.
4 Explain that you are going to give the class a problem to solve. The teams will compete to see which can suggest the most solutions to the problem at the end of five minutes. Group members will call out their ideas and the secretary will write them on the poster paper. Stress the rules for brainstorming:

1.15

LANGUAGE FOCUS
Oral practice

LEVEL
Intermediate +

TIME
20 minutes

MATERIALS
Poster size sheets of white paper and felt tip pens.

PREPARATION
None

- All the ideas must be written up.
- No questions, no discussion until the brainstorm is over.
- Tell the students to shout out ideas as they come into their heads and not to worry if they sound silly.

5 Describe the problem:

Imagine we are survivors from a plane crash in the Pacific Ocean. We have swum to a desert island and here we are, sitting on the beach, thinking what to do next. We have absolutely nothing except the clothes we are wearing. Suddenly we see something floating in the water! We run to get it. It's a case. What's inside? . . . Twenty-four cans of Coca-Cola! The problem is, what are we going to do with them? How many uses for them can you think of in five minutes?

6 At the end of the brainstorm, allow time for the students to clarify their ideas. Help to reformulate the language if it seems necessary, then come together and work out the scores.

7 Teams read out their ideas in turn and score one point for each proposal that the others didn't think of.

EXTENSION

For a follow-up, continue the simulation. Have the class debate what they ought to do with the case of Coca-Cola and come to a decision. The issues which can come out of this discussion include that of whether, in the circumstances, it's better for everybody to work together or to go their own way. The final objective of the simulation, which can include projects such as drawing the map of the island and elaborating character profiles of the survivors, is to make a plan of action for the next day on the island.

NOTES

Ideas on how to develop this kind of drama work abound in the description of the methods of Dorothy Heathcote in *Dorothy Heathcote: Drama as a Learning Medium* (Wagner 1979).

A BLIND GUEST

An information exchange activity in an imaginary situation which gives the communication a sense of urgency. There is also an awareness element which can lead to rewarding discussion.

Procedure

1 Have the students sit side by side in pairs.
2 Set the scene with a monologue something like the following:

> First I'm going to talk to the person on the left in every pair. I'm going to ask you to close your eyes and keep them closed from now until the end of the activity. Close your eyes now.
>
> Now I'm speaking to the other person in each pair. Imagine that you are at home, waiting for a friend to arrive, a person who is coming to your house for the first time and who is going to stay for a few weeks. Your friend is blind. When he (it's a man) comes, you must show him around the house and describe it to him, tell him everything that you think a blind person will need to know. Think about your home for a minute and all the information you are going to give the blind friend.
>
> Ah! There's the door bell! Take the arm of your partner. This is your friend. Tell him all about your house. The blind person, listen! If you don't understand something you must ask; be sure you have a mental picture of the place where you are going to stay. Begin now.

3 Without leaving their seats, the students talk their partners through the layout of their homes.
4 To sum up the language work you can ask the 'blind' partner to make a sketch map of the house they heard described and check through the ways of expressing spatial relationships in English.

Another possibility is to develop the theme of blindness. Opening questions for a class discussion might be: *Did you feel what it's like to be blind? Did you feel what it's like to help the blind?* It's interesting for the group to explore the amount of sensitivity different hosts showed for the needs of the blind person, through the details they described (or didn't) – the radio? the stove and coffee-making things? etc.

NOTES

We found this activity flops if you ask the students to change roles and repeat the situation.

1.16

LANGUAGE FOCUS
Describing the layout of a house or flat, oral practice

LEVEL
Lower intermediate +

TIME
20–25 minutes

MATERIALS
None

PREPARATION
None

1.17

LANGUAGE FOCUS
Oral practice

LEVEL
Intermediate

TIME
10 minutes

MATERIALS
None

PREPARATION
None

BULLS AND BEARS

A negotiating game which generates hectic discussion; an excellent way to raise energy at the start of a lesson. You need an open space to do this activity comfortably.

Procedure

1 Divide the class into three teams. Each team has a home base in a different corner of the room.

2 Explain the rules; this is a competitive game played over a number of rounds. Each round has the same pattern.

The groups retire to their home base. Each must decide whether in this round they want to be Bulls or Bears.

The teams then confront each other in the centre of the room and at a given signal simultaneously mime their animal. The Bulls make horns and tread the ground with one hoof. The Bears snarl and claw the air with their front paws.

At this point you take the score. If there are two groups with the same animal and the third with a different one, the groups in the majority score one point and the minority group scores zero. If all the teams have chosen the same animal, there is no score.

After each confrontation the groups return to their corners to discuss their tactic for the next round. Allow two minutes for them to decide and then call them to the middle.

3 The game continues in this way until one team reaches five points and is declared the winner.

1.18

LANGUAGE FOCUS
Writing

LEVEL
Elementary +

TIME
15–20 minutes

MATERIALS
Tape recorder, two pieces of music of your choice, two worksheets per student (see below)

MUSICAL CHARACTERS

A writing activity which, because of the non-verbal stimulus and the split-level worksheet, can be used with classes from elementary to advanced level.

PREPARATION

Choose two pieces of instrumental music which you guess will be unfamiliar to your students but which will make an impact on them. The greater the contrast between the two pieces, the more interesting the activity. Select an extract of two to three minutes from each. Copy the worksheet on page 25.

Procedure

1 Hand out the worksheets, two per student.

2 Tell the class they are going to fill in the questionnaires for people they don't know but whom they are going to hear described. The description is slightly unusual – it's in music. The students must imagine the person the music could represent and write an outline of them using the worksheet.

A personal record form

Part 1

Male/Female: Nationality:
Age: Height:
Profession: Hair colour:
Eye colour: Other distinguishing marks:

Part 2

Please write any other information concerning physical appearance, personality, family, habits, etc.

© Longman Group UK Ltd 1990

3 Play the first piece of music once. Allow students time to write.
4 Then play it again and pause a little longer.
5 Play it a third time and wait for the class to finish writing.
6 Compare the results in groups (allows more discussion of detail) or all together (gives a bigger pool of ideas).
7 Repeat the procedure for the second piece of music. In the final discussion ask the students to focus on the differences between the two characters they have written about.

EXTENSION

The activity can be extended into drama. First have the students reinforce the characters they imagined by walking around the room in role to the music, projecting their persona through movement. Do this for both pieces of music, then ask the learners to imagine that fate in some way brought the two musical characters together. Go around the class listening to the stories that the students think of to connect the characters. Pick up one of these and ask two people from the group to roleplay a meeting between them, with the student who made the story acting as director.

NOTES

It's not necessary to search out music composed specifically to describe people.

1.19

LANGUAGE FOCUS
Oral Practice

LEVEL
Intermediate

TIME
30 minutes

MATERIALS
Tape recorder, with independent microphone if possible, blank cassette

PREPARATION
None

A JOURNEY

A drama technique for creating a narrative based on the collective experience of an imaginary journey. If you have lots of space to work in the activity is easier, but it's possible to do it in the corridors between rows of desks. The role of teacher in this activity is leader-by-example, which makes it different from many of the ideas in this book which ask the teacher to facilitate, observe and support.

Procedure

In the first part of the activity you communicate to the class without speaking.

1 Beckon to the students. Have them leave their places and join you at the front of the class.
2 Make a gesture and show that they must copy it. Establish in this way that they must do everything that you do.
3 When this is clear, lead the students in Indian file on an imaginary journey, through adventures that you will mime and they will imitate. You might for instance:

Set off with long, confident strides,
Leap over a running stream,
Pick your way over loose boulders,
Climb slowly up a winding mountain track,
Walk through snow,
Put your head down and advance with tiny steps into the teeth of a gale,
Scramble down a hillside,
Hide from wild animals,
Wade through deep mud,
Rest,
See your destination in the distance,
Run the last few metres,
Sigh with relief when you finally arrive.

4 At the end of this phase have the students sit in a circle and place the tape recorder in the middle. Suggest to the group that now the journey is over it would be a good idea to record something of the experience. Say that you will begin and then ask the students to continue.
5 Set the tape machine to 'record' with the 'pause' button down. Lift the 'pause' and begin the story:

Our journey began on the morning of April 1st, 19___.
The weather was fine and the road was good.

Put the 'pause' button down again.
6 The next person to speak practises their contribution with the help of the teacher if necessary, and then lifts the 'pause', records their part

of the story and puts the button down again. Continuing in this way you record an uninterrupted narrative without any language errors.

7 Finish by playing back the whole recording.

MONSTERS

A game for revising names of the parts of the body. The element of the absurd has the serious purpose of helping to make new language memorable.

Procedure

1 Have everybody take five small slips of paper and write on each one word for a part of the body.
2 Divide the class into groups of three or four.
3 Each group collects together its slips of paper and exchanges them with another.
4 The task now is for the students in each group to work together to make a picture of an animal which has all the physical features listed on the slips of paper. No words can be discarded, so if a group finds it has the word *nose* seven times the animal must have seven noses.
5 When the animal picture is complete, the group write a short profile under the following headings:

Height
Weight
Habitat
Diet
Mating habits
Call/cry
Social habits
Name

© Longman Group UK Ltd 1990

6 Post the pictures around the room. Re-distribute the profiles at random and ask groups to match the pictures and descriptions.

1.20

LANGUAGE FOCUS
Vocabulary revision, oral practice

LEVEL
Elementary – lower intermediate

TIME
20 minutes

MATERIALS
Pen and paper

PREPARATION
None

CHAPTER 2

Exercises

WORD RELATIONS

LANGUAGE FOCUS
Vocabulary revision

LEVEL
Beginner +

TIME
10 minutes

MATERIALS
Pen and paper, a
cardboard box

This is an exercise in categorising by metaphor which asks students to find the same relationships between words as between different members of a family.

PREPARATION

Make a list of the vocabulary you want to revise. You will need the same number of words as students in the class. Write each word on a small piece of paper and put all the pieces in the box.

Procedure

1 Students leave their places and come together in an open space.
2 They each take one word from the box, memorise it and put it in their pocket (don't accept questions about meanings at this point but talk to students who need help individually during the next stage).
3 Explain that the object is to move around, share the words and form pairs or groups according to the following instructions.
4 Call out the instructions below one by one, stopping to hear the results of each task. Keep the activity moving briskly (don't wait for the whole class to find a pair or group each time). Don't insist on rigid linguistic criteria (e.g. *synonymy, hyponymy, antonymy, collocation*) for the categorising. Leave room for the students' interpretation of the metaphors. Here is the list of instructions (which can be added to):
   - Find a group of words (at least three) which make a family.
   - Find pairs of words which are: Fathers and sons
     Twins
     Husbands and wives
     Husbands and mothers-in-law

NOTES

The principle of grouping vocabulary with the help of metaphors is from *Vocabulary* (Morgan and Rinvolucri 1986).

SCRAMBLED DICTATIONS

A technique for presenting new vocabulary which develops students' implicit knowledge of the shape of English words. The exercise provides good spelling practice and has the excitement of discovery associated with code-breaking.

Procedure

1 Spell out the words for the students to write down, giving the letters in a scrambled sequence. For example:

ERIGNGS   NGIR   UPN   FTAD
EETAS   ITW   ROCHTLE   YZAN

The point of the exercise always depends on the students not having seen the vocabulary before.

2 Ask the students to decode the words. Their object is to find the combination of letters which is most likely to form an English word or words (students may make more than one for each group of letters).
3 Put the learners in groups of three to compare solutions.
4 Then ask the students to read the text for the lesson and as they go through the passage hunt for the words that you dictated in code.
5 After the reading, check the results all together. How many of the words did the class find? Look at any non-existent 'words' that the students made and distinguish between admissable and inadmissable spelling combinations.

VARIATIONS

A variation is to dictate phrases or short sentences from a text in scrambled sequence and have students find the correct word order.

2.2

LANGUAGE FOCUS
Spelling of new vocabulary

LEVEL
Beginner +

TIME
5–10 minutes

MATERIALS
Pen and paper, a reading text for the lesson

PREPARATION
Select the key words that you want to present from the text

MNEMONICS

This activity has the explicit objective of helping students memorise (as opposed to remember) new vocabulary. Introduce it after the presentation of words which the students will need to use during the rest of the lesson.

Procedure

1 Divide the board into two equal parts with a vertical line. On the left hand side write the new vocabulary (up to fifteen items) in a scatter pattern. Leave the other side blank.
2 Take one item of vocabulary at a time and ask the class to suggest a trigger word for it. The trigger word must be something 'easy' which the students learned as beginners and which starts with the same letter as the word they want to remember.

2.3

LANGUAGE FOCUS
Vocabulary, memory

LEVEL
Intermediate +

TIME
5 minutes

MATERIALS
Black/whiteboard

PREPARATION
None

3 Put the trigger words on the right hand side of the board, again in a scatter pattern and every time you write one up rub out its partner on the opposite side of the board. In this way, by the end of this stage, the right hand side is full and the left is blank.

4 Now go through the process in reverse. For each of the trigger words ask the students to recall the new item of vocabulary and write it on the left.

5 When you have all the new lexis again, clean the board completely and go on with the next part of the lesson.

2.4

LANGUAGE FOCUS
Pronunciation

LEVEL
Intermediate

TIME
20–25 minutes

MATERIALS
Pen and paper

PREPARATION
None

PRONUNCIATION CLINIC

An activity for intermediate level which helps students resolve doubts about standard pronunciations by analysing each other's speech.

1 Get students into pairs, sitting face to face with pens and note pads at the ready. Ask each individual to think of a topic they would like to talk to their partners about for two or three minutes.

2 Students take turns to speak, while their partners listen and take notes. The listeners' job is to write down any word the speakers pronounce in a way which they think is different from the way they themselves say it.
(Note: You are not asking students to judge what is correct, but to notice differences between idiolects.) The listeners must not interrupt.

3 At the end of the monologue the partners look together at the notes and discuss them. Be available to answer queries and especially to distinguish between what is an acceptable (comprehensible) variation in pronunciation and what is simply incorrect.

4 Have students change over roles and repeat the exercise.

5 Continue, changing roles after each monologue for as long as you have time. Often the first listening does not bring to light many significant issues, but the longer the exercise goes on the more the students get from it.

NOTES

This exercise is especially useful for multi-national classes, but need not be confined to learners with different first languages.

SYNTAX

An exercise in sentence construction with a problem-solving approach.

Procedure

1 Explain the task: you are going to dictate a sentence and the students are going to write it in an unusual way. Instead of going horizontally across the page they must write the words vertically, one under the other, in four columns (see below).

2 Dictate the sentence, telling the students when to begin a new column.

3 The aim now is to fill the horizontal spaces with a word or words which will combine with the existing ones to make a complete text. The choice of topic is up to the students. The text can be divided into any number of sentences, but they must be related and the passage as a whole has to have meaning as well as being grammatically and syntactically correct. Students work individually or in pairs.

4 To finish, put the frame on the board and compare different student texts (coloured chalk/board markers are useful to distinguish the insertions). As far as possible give students the responsibility for deciding the acceptability of a proposed solution.

Here is an example of a frame The sentence is from *Teaching Languages: A Way and Ways* by Earl Stevick (Newbury House 1980):

Why	of	demanding	the
then	teaching	of	same
undertake	which	skill	time
a	is	and	so
kind	so	at	risky

Here is an example of a student text from an upper-intermediate class.

2.5

LANGUAGE FOCUS
Writing

LEVEL
Beginner +

TIME
10–15 minutes

MATERIALS
Black/whiteboard, pen and paper

PREPARATION
Choose a sentence with at least twelve words from a text you have studied in class recently

Car s *do not*	have *any*	hope .*Although it's difficult*	to *tell their*
owners *that they've*	been *banging their heads*	against *a wall,*	their *future is*
in *danger,*	given *the situation today.*	*I*ncreased *pollution and*	parking *chaos are*
old *problems which call for*	a *dramatic change.*	*C*harges *for access to*	areas *where people usually*
park *are a*	ray *of hope*	for	
road *lovers:*	A soft	entrance *to a new future!*	

Fig. 3

2.6

LANGUAGE FOCUS
Revision of tenses,
oral practice

LEVEL
Intermediate +

TIME
10–15 minutes

MATERIALS
None

PREPARATION
None

A TENSES REVIEW

This is an activity which gives students the opportunity to review the tenses they know and work on any areas of difficulty.

Procedure

1 One student leaves the room and prepares a number of questions to ask the group on a subject of their choice.
2 Meanwhile the rest of the class decide on a tense they want to practise.
3 When the tense is agreed they call the other student back into the room.
4 This student asks the questions prepared outside, directing them to individuals in the class. The students answer and in every reply they must include an example of the practice tense. The questioner's task is to guess which tense this is, while the class must try to camouflage it in the answers so it is not immediately obvious. The dialogue continues until the questioner identifies the target tense.
5 The teacher, who in the meantime has been noting any areas of confusion, reports back to the group and goes through any corrections which are necessary.
6 Another student then leaves the room and the exercise continues for the number of rounds you and the students feel is useful.

2.7

LANGUAGE FOCUS
Sentence
construction

LEVEL
Elementary

TIME
10 minutes

MATERIALS
'Cuisinaire rods'
(small set) or strips
of coloured card

SENTENCES IN RODS

A sentence structure exercise for pairs, using 'Cuisinaire rods' or strips of card of different lengths and colours to represent relationships between pairs of words (*I – me; do – does; he – him*) and to distinguish between others (*I – you – he*). The activity is interesting for students only if the target structures are new, so that in the course of their experiments with the language they discover sentences which they have never seen before. If the language is already familiar, the exercise loses this problem-solving element. The example we give below is a task we have used with learners in their first ten hours of English.

PREPARATION

Make a list of the components of the structure(s) you want the students to explore – ten or twelve is about the right number. Match each element with a rod to make a key, as shown in Fig. 4.

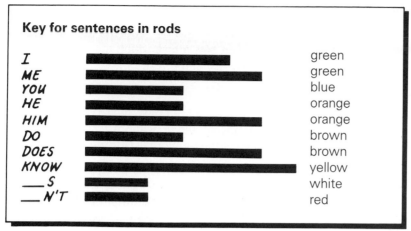

Key for sentences in rods

I		green
ME		green
YOU		blue
HE		orange
HIM		orange
DO		brown
DOES		brown
KNOW		yellow
___S		white
___N'T		red

Fig. 4

Procedure

1 Pair the students.
2 Give each pair the 'Key', together with a number of rods of the lengths and colours you have selected (the more rods, the longer the exercise lasts).
3 Explain the task: one student places the rods end to end to make a 'sentence' and the partner uses the key to decode it and read it out aloud. Taking turns at composing sentences, the students continue in this way until they can find no new permutations.

VARIATIONS

To introduce a competitive edge, introduce the rule that the winner is the student in the pair who is able to find the last sentence (no repetition is allowed, and all sentences must be meaningful and correct).

2.8

LANGUAGE FOCUS
Listening, reading

LEVEL
Elementary +

TIME
15–20 minutes

MATERIALS
Tape recording of a song, 'runtogethertext'

RUNTOGETHERTEXTS

An activity to use with songs which allows the students the support of the written word as they listen, but sets a task which makes them read intelligently, focusing on the structure of the text.

PREPARATION

Take the text of a song your learners will not have heard or read before and rewrite it as if it were one long sentence, without any punctuation. For example, this traditional song sung by Woodie Guthrie.

Come all you old time cowboys and listen to my song please do not grow weary for I will not detain you long it is concerning some wild cowboys who did agree to go and spend the summer pleasant on the trail of the buffalo I found myself in Griffin in 1883 a famous well-known drover he addressed himself to me he said how do you do young fellow and how would you like to go and spend the summer pleasant on the trail of the buffalo me being out of work right then to the drover I did say this going out on the buffalo range depends on your pay if you pay good wages and transportation too I reckon I might go with you on the trail of the buffalo of course I pay good wages and transportation too if you agree to come with me and see the season through but if you do get homesick and try to run away you will starve to death out on the trail and you will also lose your pay well with all his flattering talking he assembled quite a team there were ten or twelve of us all able-bodied men our trip it was a pleasant one as we crossed the western trail until we came to Bogie Creek down in old New Mexico there our pleasures ended and our troubles all began a lightning storm hit and made the cattle run we got all full of stickers from the cactus that did grow and the outlaws waiting to pick us off on the trail of the buffalo well when the season ended the drover would not pay he said you should not have drunk so much you are all in debt to me well we cowboys never heard of no fancy bankrupt law so we left the drover's bones to bleach out on the trail of the buffalo

© Longman Group UK Ltd 1990

Make one copy per student.

Procedure

1 Without any explanation, hand out the texts and ask for volunteers to read it out aloud. If the students don't make sense of it at first, persevere until they grasp the fact that they have to space the text and realise that it is probably a poem or a song.
2 At this point, play the recording of the song and have the students mark the line and verse endings as they listen.
3 Compare results in pairs and then listen again for confirmation.

EXTENSION

Follow this activity with whatever text or language work you have in mind for the song.

VARIATIONS

Amoredifficultbutveryinterestingvariationistoprepareatextwithnogaps betweenthewordsandaskthestudentstodecipherit.

A GRAMMATICAL COLLAGE

A sentence structure exercise similar to Activity 2.7 (p. 32) in that it encourages an adventurous, experimental approach towards grammar and syntax, and generates an enormous volume of language.

PREPARATION

Snip words from newsprint at random to make a collage similar to the one in Fig. 5. Different type faces and styles make a more interesting visual effect, which is important, since the students will be working intensively on the page for some time. Photocopy the collage for every pair in the class.

Fig. 5

2.9

LANGUAGE FOCUS
Sentence construction

LEVEL
Beginner +

TIME
15 minutes

MATERIALS
A grammar collage for each pair in the group (see Fig. 5)

Procedure

1 Students work in pairs. Ask them to find the shortest sentence they can using only the words from the collage, and write it down.

2 Now ask them to find a sentence with one word more than the first sentence, and then to continue in their own time to make sentences one word longer than the previous one for as long as they can. A word which appears only once in the collage can appear only once in any sentence, but can be used in any number of sentences.

VARIATIONS

The exercise can be turned into a competition in a number of ways, for example, by aiming to find the most sentences in a given time or make the longest sentence.

NOTES

This activity is inspired by the work of Caleb Gattegno.

2.10

LANGUAGE FOCUS
Structure revision: question forms

LEVEL
Elementary +

TIME
10–15 minutes

MATERIALS
One worksheet for each pair of students

FIND THE QUESTIONS

Another way to exploit the word collage principle, this time with a puzzle element.

PREPARATION

Choose seven questions which exemplify structures you want the class to revise and write a short example sentence for each, on the same topic. Write the words from your seven questions in a random scatter pattern on a plain white sheet of paper, without using capital letters or punctuation. Number blank lines below the collage down the left hand margin, from one to seven. See page 37. Photocopy this page for every pair in the class.

Procedure

1 In class students work in pairs to re-form your original sentences, or find new ones. They must not add or change words, use words in the collage more than once or leave any out.

2 Allow five minutes to work on the problem, then put pairs together to pool ideas and finish off the task (this helps students from getting blocked).

NOTES

This activity can also be used as an individual homework task.

Find the questions about newspapers

you   got   did   which   always
        do   your   your   page   the
do   Sundays   how   about   what
    reads   the   you   in   you
prefer   when   papers   read   today
            a   favourite
paper   is   who   house   one
buy   paper   do   newspaper   you

1 _____

2 _____

3 _____

4 _____

5 _____

6 _____

7 _____

THE LISTENING CHAIN

2.11

An intensive listening and pronunciation activity with a self-correcting mechanism, based on discrimination of minimal pairs. The exercise needs total concentration and disciplined cooperation in the group.

PREPARATION
The first time you do the activity, copy the set of cards reproduced on the next page. You need one set for every group of five students. When you are familiar with the exercise you can design materials for the special needs of your class.

Procedure

Demonstrate the exercise with one group before giving it to the whole class.

LANGUAGE FOCUS
Listening, pronunciation

LEVEL
Intermediate +

TIME
10–15 minutes

MATERIALS
One set of listening cards for every group of five students

1 Have the students sit in a circle, not too close together. Hand out the listening cards. Explain the rules which the group must respect at all costs:
- You must not show your card to anyone else.
- The only words you can speak for the duration of the exercise are those written on the cards.

1

HEAR	SAY
fin	1. clothes
van	sock
ice-cream	Don't! Go away!
a blackbird	pot
	wander

2

HEAR	SAY
close	light
thin	heart
Don't! Go away!	ice-cream
pot	a blackbird

3

HEAR	SAY
clothes	pull
officers	van
Don't go away!	spots
port	carpet
wonder	wrong

4

HEAR	SAY
pull	thin
art	plum
offices	today
a black bird	baby

5

HEAR	SAY
pool	plant
heart	officers
fan	lorry
scream	police
wander	finish

2 The activity proceeds in the following way: the student who has the number 1 next to a word in the 'Say' column of their card begins by

reading out this word. The rest of the group search the 'Hear' column of their cards for the word the first student said. The one who finds it must read the word opposite it, in the 'Say' column. The others look on their cards in the 'Hear' column for the last word that was spoken and the student who finds it continues the chain by saying the corresponding word in the 'Say' column. Using the set of cards shown on page 38, the exercise begins in the following way:

STUDENT 1: *Clothes!*
STUDENT 3: *Pull!*
STUDENT 4: *Thin!*
STUDENT 2: *Heart!*

The sequence continues in this way until student 5 reads the last word which is *finish*. It is inevitable, however, that on occasions students will mistake a word they hear for the other one of the minimal pair. In this case they will break the chain by reading out a word which does not reappear on another card. You know the chain is broken when silence follows the last word which was read out. When this happens the group must go back to the beginning and start again. The students are not allowed to repeat a word when it's their turn to speak – insist on this rule or the exercise will disintegrate.

3 When the procedure is clear to everybody, swap around the cards in the demonstration group, hand out the materials to the rest of the class and let the students practise the exercise by themselves.

NOTES

The frustration of the continually breaking chain motivates the students to enormous efforts at communication.

The principle of the listening chain was taught to us by Denny Packard and was developed by Krys Markowski.

THE SPELLING BOX

A remedial activity which can help to resolve specific difficulties related to spelling and pronunciation.

PREPARATION

Before class, choose a number of spelling-sound combinations which cause difficulty for your learners. Write these letters in a cube with nine boxes, as in the centre of Fig. 7, and experiment until you find the cube that spells the words you want to focus on.

Procedure

1 Write your cube on the board.
2 Tell the students to make as many words as possible with these

2.12

LANGUAGE FOCUS
Spelling,
pronunciation

LEVEL
Elementary – lower-
intermediate

TIME
10 minutes

MATERIALS
Black/whiteboard

letters in three minutes. Words can be of any length. They can only use the letters in the cube. They cannot use twice in the same word a letter which appears in the cube only once. Students should write the words they find in a scatter pattern on a piece of note paper.

3 When time is up, have two volunteers come to the board and write up the words from the cube that the rest of the class dictate to them. These again should be written in a scatter pattern around the spelling box. Students add to their own solutions any words that they didn't think of.

4 When all the words have been collected, pair the students and ask them to classify the words according to their pronunciation. In this example, the focus is on central vowel sounds. Demonstrate a system for denoting rhyming words, like the one in Fig. 6.

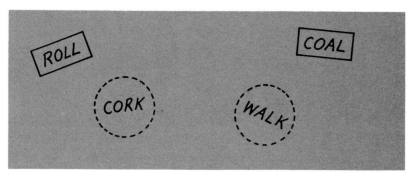

Fig. 6

5 When the pairs have had time to finish the task, get the class to put the solution on the board (see Fig. 7 below).

Fig. 7

NOTES

There is a double point to the exercise: students get practice in transcribing sounds correctly in Step 3 when they dictate to each other (sound to word). They then work in the opposite direction when they have to classify the rhymes by reading (word to sound).

SELECTIVE LISTENING (1)

Three exercises to use on different occasions, grouped together because they accompany the same kind of texts and have the same objective, that of developing intensive listening comprehension. Although the techniques involve an element of dictation, you use much more difficult texts than you would normally dictate. You need a passage delivered at natural speed that your class will be able to pick out words and phrases from without being able to transcribe it all or understand all the details at a first listening. Tape-recorded intensive listening passages from modern EFL course books are ideal. Add one of these activities to the exercises that accompany the cassette.

PREPARATION

For all the tasks you need a passage of eighty to a hundred words, with a transcript. Number the sentences/utterances.

Procedure

Students write down the left-hand margin of an exercise page the numbers of sentences/utterances in the text. Play the passage, pausing at the end of each sentence/utterance. The students must write the third word they hear in each line. Review the results and work on any areas of difficulty (probably ellision and contraction).

2.13

LANGUAGE FOCUS
Listening

LEVEL
Beginner +

TIME
5–15 minutes
(depending on the task)

MATERIALS
Tape recorder, authentic/simulated recorded listening passage

SELECTIVE LISTENING (2)

PREPARATION

For all the tasks you need a passage of eighty to a hundred words, with a transcript. Number the sentences/utterances.

Procedure

Give each student one word from the passage, written on a slip of paper. They must be words which appear only once in the text. As the students listen to the tape, they must pick out their own word and write it down, together with those which come immediately before and after it on the tape. Use these fragments to reconstruct the passage.

2.14

LANGUAGE FOCUS
Listening

LEVEL
Beginner +

TIME
5–15 minutes
(depending on the task)

MATERIALS
Tape recorder, authentic/simulated recorded listening passage

2.15

LANGUAGE FOCUS
Listening

LEVEL
Beginner +

TIME
5–15 minutes
(depending on the
task)

MATERIALS
Tape recorder,
authentic/simulated
recorded listening
passage

SELECTIVE LISTENING (3)

PREPARATION

For all the tasks you need a passage of eighty to a hundred words, with a transcript. Number the sentences/utterances.

Procedure

Divide the class into teams of three. Students number down the left hand margin as in Activity 2.13 above, and listen to the sentences/utterances one at a time. The first person in a team writes down everything they can grasp of the beginning of each line, the second person writes the middle, and the third the end. The students then put the three parts together to reconstruct the sentences/utterances. Leave it to the students to decide what is the beginning, middle and end of the sentence/utterance as they listen, and notice how they perceive segments.

2.16

LANGUAGE FOCUS
Sentence structure,
writing

LEVEL
Beginner +

TIME
20 minutes

MATERIALS
One (different)
newspaper photo for
each pair of students,
one worksheet for
each pair (see below)

CAPTIONS

An activity for structure revision using newspaper photos, a challenging and fun way to get students to write practice sentences.

PREPARATION

1 Write out seven or eight sentence beginnings of structures you want the class to practise. Photocopy for each pair.
2 Cut out a lively newspaper photo for every two students. Each pair needs a different picture.

Procedure

1 Form pairs, sitting side by side.
2 Hand out the worksheet. On page 43 is an example you might use with an intermediate group:
3 Hand out the photos and explain the task: each pair must write a caption for their photo using each of the sentence beginnings in turn. Pairs then compare their work with another pair, check for grammatical correctness and explain allusions. To finish, each pair presents to the class the captions written by the other which they find most interesting.

I wish I'd never . . .
How would you like . . .
It's the first time I've ever . . .
Perhaps I should have . . .
If I were you . . .
Supposing I . . .
Unless I . . .
I doubt if . . .

© Longman Group UK Ltd 1990

PROGRESSIVE CLOZE

Not so much an activity in its own right as a technique you can incorporate into your blackboard work. Use this idea to consolidate grammatical structures you have been presenting on the board.

Procedure

1 Choose a sentence that you have written on the board and that you want the class to focus on. You need a continuous piece of text of fifteen to twenty words. Clean everything else from the board.
2 Ask one student to read out aloud the model text.
3 Rub out two words from the middle of the text and ask another to reconstruct the whole text.
4 Rub out more words on either side of the space. Ask another student to say the whole text.
5 Continue in this way until there are no words left on the board and the class has to remember the entire text.

2.17

LANGUAGE FOCUS
Consolidation of grammatical forms

LEVEL
Beginner +

TIME
3 minutes

MATERIALS
Black/whiteboard

PREPARATION
None

2.18

LANGUAGE FOCUS
Question forms,
writing, intensive
reading

LEVEL
Beginner +

TIME
30 minutes

MATERIALS
Copies of the reading
passage for every
student, pen and
paper

PREPARATION
None

PERSONALISED COMPREHENSION QUESTIONS

This is a student-centred alternative to conventional reading comprehension exercises which you can use with classes at any level. The aim
is not only to find out (i.e. test) what students have learned (or not
learned) from a reading passage, but also to discover the kinds of things
they *want* to learn. In our experience, students read more closely and
find out more from a text when they write questions on it than when
they have to answer them. You can select passages especially for this
exercise or use those from the course book you are following.

Procedure

1 Get the class into groups of five or six and have each group sit around
a table.
2 Ask the students to study the reading passage silently.
3 They then work together in their groups to write one question about
the text for each member of the group sitting at the next table. Each
question must be written on a separate piece of paper and begin with
the name of the person to whom it is addressed. Stress the import-
ance of writing questions with a particular person in mind, but leave
it to the students to decide the type of questions to ask.
4 The questions are then passed to the people they were written for,
who work individually on writing the answers, referring to the text if
they wish.
5 When everybody has finished, students work within their groups and
read out their questions and the answers they gave to them. Allow
time for discussion.
6 Finally, bring the class together and ask the learners to share
questions they received which they found particularly interesting or
difficult. Be prepared to answer queries about the correctness of
students' answers.

TITLES

A creative writing exercise using pictures.

PREPARATION

1 Select the pictures to work with. Abstract or semi-abstract paintings work better than representational ones for this purpose. Have the postcards ready, but don't show them until Step 3.
2 Prepare a slip of paper for each pair of students with the titles of four of the pictures. There must be one title on every slip which is unique to that group, while the others can be used any number of times. Mix up the titles at random, and write them without punctuation. Here are some examples:

the young english girl
person looking at the sun
girls on the bridge
afternoon encounter
air, iron and water
enigma of an autumn evening
study
the poor fisherman
the path up through the field
nude
summer steps
inflexible
women on the beach
persistence of memory
the house of the hanged man
elasticity

Procedure

1 Pair the students sitting side by side and give each pair a slip of paper with four titles as prepared. Do not say anything about what the slips are or where they come from.
2 The task is to write a short text (a 'text' can be a paragraph of prose or a piece of free verse) which incorporates all the words/phrases on the paper. The titles can appear in any order, but the students must not change them or break them up. Encourage the class to work quickly and not to spend a lot of time rewriting.
3 When everyone has finished, spread out the postcards on a table or the floor and have students choose a picture to illustrate their writing. Pairs who want the same postcard must negotiate.
4 To finish, students present their work to the whole class.

2.19

LANGUAGE FOCUS
Writing

LEVEL
Intermediate –
advanced

TIME
30 minutes

MATERIALS
Postcard
reproductions of
modern paintings,
one for each pair of
students

2.20

LANGUAGE FOCUS
Writing

LEVEL
Beginner +

TIME
10–15 minutes

MATERIALS
Pen and paper

CONCRETE WRITING

This is a way to get students to take an interest in writing. The unusual instruction gives the important initial impulse which makes all the difference to the state of motivation in which the students approach the task. If your class has no energy for composition writing, this could be a technique to try. The interesting visual effect of the completed work gives a sense of satisfaction. From the writing skills point of view this exercise encourages the kind of fluent, unselfconscious expression which rarely emerges from the conventional, structured essay form.

PREPARATION

Think of a simple image that will represent the topic that you want the students to write about.

Procedure

1 Don't mention the forthcoming writing task. Describe your prepared image to your students and simply ask them to draw an *outline* picture of your chosen image. The size (half page, page, double page) depends on the amount you want the students to write, but should be specified. There mustn't be any details drawn inside the outline.
2 Give the students the title of the writing assignment and tell them to write it above the picture.
3 They then write their composition on the topic using the space inside the drawing, starting at the top and finishing when they have no more room.
4 Post the work on the walls.

NOTES

Topics which have worked well with this technique include 'Nuclear power' (inside a mushroom cloud) and 'Me' (inside a profile of the student's face).

CHAPTER 3

Conversations

LINE-UPS

A group task with many variations that gives beginners the satisfaction of organising themselves using simple utterances in the target language and helps establish the group identity at the start of a course.

Procedure

1 Ask students to make a line, standing shoulder to shoulder, in order of the day and month of their birthdays. Use the space you have, at the front of the class, around the walls or in the corridors between the desks and help the group by establishing the points where the line starts (January) and finishes (December).
2 When the task has been completed get the students to call out their birthdays in sequence to check the line.

VARIATIONS

A challenging variation for the group is to form the line with eyes closed.

The line-up technique can be used for numerous simple information exchanges such as:

Alphabetical order of christian names
The time you go to bed/have lunch/get up
The distance from your home to the school
Age
A date which is special for you

Used in a string, one after the other, line-ups are a quick, effective way for new groups to find out basic information about themselves. On the other hand, topics such as 'A date which is special for you' can lead to a fuller conversation and are best done sitting, in a circle.

3.1

LANGUAGE FOCUS
Dates, oral practice

LEVEL
Beginner –
elementary

TIME
5 minutes

MATERIALS
None

PREPARATION
None

3.2

LANGUAGE FOCUS
Writing, discussion

LEVEL
Lower
intermediate +

TIME
15–20 minutes

MATERIALS
Pen and paper

PREPARATION
None

WHO AM I?

An exercise in inventiveness which gives the opportunity to exchange personal information.

Procedure

1 Everyone (include yourself if you and your students feel comfortable sharing personal information) takes a page of A4 paper and divides it in two, horizontally.

2 In the top half, draw a self-portrait.

3 In the bottom half, get the class to complete a sentence beginning *I am* ... in nine different ways. All the sentences must be grammatically correct, true and interesting. The instruction for the task may be met with blank looks: resist the temptation to intervene and allow the students time to discover for themselves that the more they experiment with different sentence constructions the more they find they can write and the more interesting the results.

4 When everyone has finished, post the pages on the walls and have the students move about looking at the completed worksheets. Don't allow this to take so long that the activity loses momentum.

5 Sit down again and discuss what the worksheets reveal. This can be an open discussion for more advanced groups or a guided one for lower levels. The following activity is ideal for organising feedback from this task.

3.3

LANGUAGE FOCUS
Various

LEVEL
Beginner +

THE FEEDBACK ROUND

An invaluable activity for summing up almost any classroom experience, based on four simple rules:

1 Everybody in the group is allowed to speak once and only once. Students can contribute in random order, raising a hand when they want to speak or take turns in a fixed order.

2 Anybody who does not want to speak is free to remain silent. Be careful to make this clear and avoid putting pressure on students to perform. In this activity people work hard also just by listening.

3 No interrupting. No right of reply. The group must concentrate on taking in what is being said.

4 All contributions must begin in the same way with the phrase *I was interested to learn that* ... .Break in at once if this formula is not used.

VARIATIONS

Other sentence beginnings to use with this technique include:
In this lesson I have found out that . . .
I was surprised to learn that . . .
I was pleased to see that . . .
In this lesson I have understood . . .
I wonder why . . .?

A GRAMMAR ROUND

An activity to consolidate a newly presented tense.

Procedure

1 Sit students in a circle if possible (don't worry if it's not).
2 Have students write their name at the top of a new page in their notebooks (using notebooks in preference to single sheets of paper means students will have a record of the activity).
3 Ask them to pass their books to the person sitting on their left.
4 Tell the class the tense they are going to practise and check that they have the form in mind.
5 Then ask the students to write a question using this tense, addressed personally to the owner of the book they have in front of them.
6 When everyone has finished, tell them to pass the notebooks to the next person on their left and write a question in the book they receive, again addressed to its owner. They should not repeat a question which has already been written. When they have finished they pass the book on once more and so on.
7 Continue the process, always using the same tense, until the books have gone a complete circle, or, if your class is too big for this, until everyone has written twelve to fifteen questions. At the end, everyone should have their own book.
8 To review the work, ask students to share with the whole class:
   ■ any question which they think has an error in it (and correct it),
   ■ a question which surprised them,
   ■ a funny question,
   ■ a question they don't understand,
   ■ a question they can't answer,
   ■ a silly question,
   ■ a boring question
   ■ a question they would prefer not to answer,
   ■ an interesting question,
   ■ a question they would like to answer (and answer it).

3.4

LANGUAGE FOCUS
Question forms in a given tense, writing

LEVEL
Beginner +

TIME
15–20 minutes

MATERIALS
Pen and students' notebooks

PREPARATION
None

This way of going over the questions leads to deeper, more interesting discussion than simply asking students to answer them. Also, weeding out the possible meaningless questions helps to establish the standard of authenticity for future activities.

3.5

LANGUAGE FOCUS
Transformation statement/ question, writing, oral practice

LEVEL
Intermediate

TIME
15–20 minutes

MATERIALS
Pen and paper

PREPARATION
None

'I WONDER IF ANYONE . . .'

A questionnaire activity with a written and an oral part, an ideal ice-breaker for new groups.

Procedure

1 Explain the aim of the activity with an introduction something like the following:
   It's natural to be curious about the composition of the group when you find yourself together with people you haven't met before. You wonder what the others are like and perhaps whether they have anything in common with you. This activity gives you the chance to find out these things about the others in the group.
2 Get the students to copy the table.

I wonder if anyone in the group:

_____	1_____
_____	2_____
_____	3_____
_____	4_____
_____	5_____
_____	6_____
_____	7_____
_____	8_____
_____	9_____

---

3 Ask them to complete the sentence-beginning in nine different ways, with the things they are curious to know about the group.
4 When everyone is ready, the students take their worksheets and a pen and, moving around the class, ask questions to find out if in fact there is *anyone who* . . . . For example, a student who wrote: *I wonder if anyone in the group: understands this activity* would move around asking people: *Do you understand this activity?* until someone gives

the answer *Yes*. the questioner then writes the name of this person on the left of number 1 on the worksheet and goes on to the next question. In this way the students make a list of statements beginning with people's names, for example:

I wonder if anyone in the group:

José   1 understands this activity

Allow enough time for most of the students to get answers to most of their questions.

5 Then ask the group to share a) interesting things they learned about each other and b) information they couldn't find out.

NOTES

This is a variation of an activity published in *Caring and Sharing in the Foreign Language Classroom* (Moskowitz 1978).

DO-IT-YOURSELF CLOZE PASSAGE

A composition activity in two parts (over two lessons) with a homework component, which gives students the chance to explore possible differences between the way they see themselves and the way others see them.

Procedure

1 Pair each student with another student sitting in a different part of the room, but have them remain in their places.
2 Set the first task: in this part of the activity each student must write a description of their partner. Explain that physical appearance, aptitudes, personality, habits, routines, life experience and any other information they might know or deduce is all valid content. The students should aim to fill one side of A4 paper. Do not reveal what comes next in the activity.
3 Collect the compositions and correct them.
4 In the next lesson, return the work and ask the students to make a neat copy of the composition at home, with one special feature: they must omit all the adjectives and leave blank spaces where they were in the text.
5 In the lesson which follows the partners exchange compositions. Each must try to fill in the missing words in the description of themselves.

3.6

LANGUAGE FOCUS
Language of personal description, writing

LEVEL
Intermediate +

TIME
Part 1, 20–30 minutes; part 2, 10–15 minutes

MATERIALS
Pen and paper

PREPARATION
None

6 When they have finished the task, pairs sit together and compare the completed cloze passages with the originals.

7 To sum up, ask the students to each say in turn something they appreciated and something they resented in their partner's description of them.

NOTES

The activity is interesting for groups in which students know each other less well because it obliges them to think hard about their peers. In the absence of 'easy' information based on long acquaintance, the learners must rely on observation and supposition, and often discover they can write more than they suspected about a person they know only slightly. At the end of this activity people feel they know each other much better.

3.7

LANGUAGE FOCUS
Writing

LEVEL
Elementary +

TIME
15–20 minutes

MATERIALS
Pen and paper

PREPARATION
None

A PERSONAL ROUND

Another activity which exploits the motivation created by giving and receiving personal feedback. From the language point of view it's a useful revision of structures and vocabulary from a typical first year of English, but is interesting at any level.

Procedure

1 The activity is easier to organise if the class is seated in a circle or a horseshoe; arrange this if possible.

2 Ask each student to write their name at the top of a blank sheet of A4 paper.

3 They then pass the sheet to the person sitting on their left.

4 Give the instruction to write one sentence about the person whose name is at the top of the page. The open task of writing 'about' gives the scope to include physical description, personality, likes and dislikes, habits, and so on.

5 When everyone has finished, ask the students to pass the page to the left again. The student who receives it must read what has been written and then write another sentence with new information about the same person. The page is then passed on again and the process repeated.

6 The activity finishes when the pages have done a complete circle, or after twelve to fifteen sentences if your class is too big for this. In any case stop the activity if you see the energy and concentration levels falling, before the writing becomes a chore. At the end everyone should have the page written about themselves.

7 To sum up, invite people to read out from their pages:
   a any sentence which is factually incorrect,
   b any sentence which made them laugh,

c any sentence which surprised them,

d any sentence which describes something about themselves they
would like to change,

e any sentence they would not have written about themselves,

f any sentence they don't understand.

Choose the instructions for this part of the activity according to the
level of the group and allow everyone who wants to speak time to
do so, without calling on students by name.

I-YOU-WE

A quick activity to do when you want students to sum up a period of
class work of any kind, a discussion, text study, listening comprehension
or whatever. The technique aims to improve the quality of listening
between students.

Procedure

Get the students in pairs, sitting face to face. Explain that the purpose of
the activity is to exchange comments on the work you have just done.
Partners speak in turn.

a First they must each say a sentence beginning with the word *I*.

b Then they must each say a sentence beginning with the word *You*.

c Finally they must each say a sentence beginning with the word *We*.

Have one pair demonstrate to the class before the others try.

EXTENSION

This can be a starting point for group discussion. At the end of the
activity, ask the pairs to report back on the agreements and disagree-
ments which emerged through the exchanges.

3.8

LANGUAGE FOCUS
Oral practice

LEVEL
Elementary +

TIME
3 minutes

MATERIALS
None

PREPARATION
None

3.9

LANGUAGE FOCUS
Vocabulary revision,
oral practice

LEVEL
Elementary +

TIME
10 minutes

MATERIALS
Black/whiteboard,
pen and paper

PREPARATION
None

NIGHT

A brainstorm activity. In large groups brainstorms can be noisy, but the noise in itself lifts the level of enthusiasm and spontaneous participation. It's difficult to imagine a successful, quiet brainstorm. A member of a training course recently renamed this the 'Thunder Test'. This particular activity can be used as a quick vocabulary revision or ask the first stage in composition writing.

Procedure

1 If you teach in a very large room, to avoid excluding people at the back, get all the students standing together close to the board.
2 Explain that in a moment you will write one word in the centre of the board. Immediately they see this word the students must shout out the words that come into their minds, words associated in some way or another with the one you wrote on the board. You will write everything they tell you. Students must observe the following rules:
   ■ No questions
   ■ No criticism
   ■ No discussion
   The class will have three minutes to collect as much vocabulary as possible.
3 Write the word NIGHT in big block capitals in the centre of the board.
4 Write around it in a scatter pattern everything the students shout out. Don't correct, comment or censure.
5 At the end of three minutes (it could go on a little longer, but stop before this phase develops into a long, slow word search) ask the students to go back to their places.
6 Check that all the words on the board are familiar. Allow time for questions from the class about obscure associations.
7 Then get the learners to work individually on writing all the vocabulary on the board in two columns, one headed 'Frightening' and the other 'Not frightening', according to the way each individual feels about the words.
8 To conclude, students form small groups and compare their lists.

EXTENSION

As a follow-up, ask students in one half of the class to write a story including all the words from the 'Frightening' column while the other half does the same with the 'Not frightening' words. Let the students choose their own theme; the subject can be anything *except* 'Night'.

GRAPH OF THE MONTH

An activity for sharing personal experiences, hence one which involves a lot of use of past tenses. The impact is greater if you can contrive to introduce this conversation at the end of the month.

PREPARATION

Before the lesson think back over the month and pick out five or six personal experiences which have made an impression on you.

Procedure

1 In class, begin the activity without an introduction. Simply ask the group to pay attention to what you write on the board.
2 First put up the graph (Fig. 8).

Fig. 8

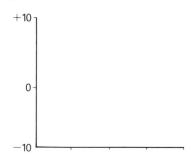

The horizontal line represents time, divided into four weeks. The vertical line gives a scale on which to evaluate your experiences, the best at the top, the worst at the bottom. (Note: *Do not* label these lines on the graph you show to your students.) Stand back and let the class look at the board for a few seconds, then, without any explanation, begin to plot your month's most significant experiences on the graph. Put a cross in the appropriate position to show how you feel about each experience and alongside it write a key word which will be a personal reminder to you of the event (but will not necessarily make sense to anyone else). Your graph will look something like Fig. 9.

Fig. 9

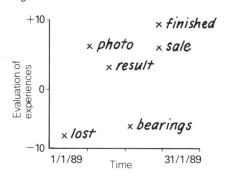

3.10

LANGUAGE FOCUS
Past tenses, oral practice

LEVEL
Intermediate +

TIME
20–30 minutes

MATERIALS
Black/whiteboard, pen and paper

3 Invite the class to tell you what they think the graph represents. Allow the group time to work it out for themselves, but if this becomes too protracted, narrate one of the experiences from your graph. Then ask the students to find out about the others by questioning you.

4 Have the students make a graph of the month for themselves, representing not fewer than five experiences. Be available to help with the key words.

5 When everyone has finished, form groups of three or four and have the students present their graphs to each other. This is a good opportunity for you to listen in to the group work without feeling you are intruding – you have shared your experiences with the class so it's natural for you to hear those of the students.

VARIATIONS

The graph technique can be used for course evaluation. Ask the students to put the best and worst lessons of the month, or the most interesting and least interesting units in the course book onto a graph.

3.11

LANGUAGE FOCUS
Language of geographical location, oral practice

LEVEL
Elementary +

TIME
5–10 minutes

MATERIALS
None

PREPARATION
None

A MAP ON THE FLOOR

A language and movement activity for groups of students all from the same country. It can be used to teach how to exchange elementary information about geographical location, but also has potential for advanced level conversation. Talking about their roots is a powerful topic for adults.

To do the activity successfully you need a fairly large open space.

Procedure

1 Have the students stand in a circle around the empty space.

2 Ask them to imagine that a map of their (or your) country has been drawn on the floor in front of them. Point out a few landmarks and show the shape of the frontiers.

3 Explain that you are going to give instructions for the students to go and stand at different places on the map. The learners must find their bearings by checking with the people around them. This creates exchanges like:
Where are you?
I'm in . . .
Where's that?
Near . . . , south of . . .
More elaborate negotiation can develop,
If this is Lyons, St Etienne must be there.
Is Beaune north or south of Dijon?
You should be a bit further west.

4 The instructions you give will depend on the age and experience of your class. Here are some suggestions for an adult group:

Go to the place(where) , , , you were born.

your father's father was born.

you spent your first holiday.

you have felt at home.

you could never live.

you would like to retire.

you will probably be buried when you die.

5 After each instruction ask different people to tell where they are, and say something about the place, but keep the activity moving briskly.

6 If you want to extend the discussion, after the last instruction ask students to sit down where they are (it's difficult to sustain a conversation standing) and tell the people near them about the places they have recalled in the last few minutes.

EXTENSION

As a follow-up, if you have students from different parts of the country, ask them to present their home towns to the group with the use of a quick sketch map on the board.

FAMILIES I

An idea for teaching family relationships through a communication gap activity.

Procedure

1 Write your name on the board and, using it as a starting point, build up your family tree step by step. Do not write the other names however, but show the existence of members of the family with a box, as in Fig. 10 on page 58.

2 Present the words for family relationships as you go along. Make a list on the board if your students are used to seeing new vocabulary written, but involve them in this list-making by having them tell you how to spell the new words before you write them, by listening to the sounds.

3 When the family tree is complete, ask the students to make a diagram of their families in the same way, writing their own names but leaving out the others.

4 Pair the students and ask them to turn their chairs back to back.

5 Have the partners exchange family trees and then explain the task: taking turns the students must ask questions to enable them to fill in the names in the empty boxes in the partner's diagram. They must not

3.12

LANGUAGE FOCUS
Family relationship words, oral practice

LEVEL
Elementary

TIME
20–30 minutes

MATERIALS
Black/whiteboard, pen and paper

PREPARATION
None

turn around or show the page they are working on until both trees are complete.

6 At this point they look at the diagrams together and check the details.

7 Ask the students to keep their own family trees for future use.

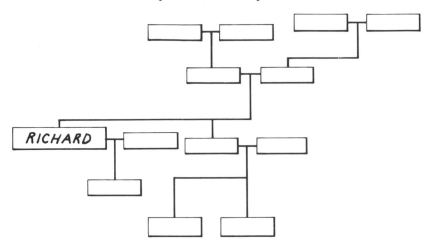

Fig. 10

3.13

LANGUAGE FOCUS
Oral practice, note-taking

LEVEL
Elementary +

TIME
15–20 minutes

MATERIALS
Pen and paper

PREPARATION
None

FAMILIES II

A possible follow-up to the previous activity, which develops more conversation around the family tree, but one that can also be used independently.

Procedure

1 Ask students to draw a family tree, or take the one prepared in the previous activity.

2 Pair the students and have them sit face to face. If you are following on from Activity 3.12, keep the same pairs.

3 Students in each pair exchange family trees.

4 Explain that in the activity they are about to do, one student in each pair will ask questions and the other will reply. Ask them to decide the roles.

5 Give the instructions: the questioner must choose four people in the partner's family and ask for four items of information about each person. The questions must be of different types. For example, if a student asks the age of one person, that question cannot be repeated later. This means that the students have to find sixteen different questions. The information gathered is written in note form under the name of the person to whom it refers on the family tree.

6 At the end of the question session, have the students go through the notes together and then change roles and repeat the task.

NOTES

The small detail of sitting face to face has a positive impact on the quality of the conversation out of all proportion to the effort requires to turn two chairs through 45°.

EXTENSION

This activity can usefully be followed by a feedback round (see Activity 3.3).

FAMILIES III

A vocabulary expansion activity which makes use of the family tree at a slightly higher language level.

Procedure

1 Ask students to draw a family tree or return to the one they made in the previous activities. When the diagram is ready have them put it to one side for a moment and focus on the blackboard.
2 Write on the board:
   G = generous
3 Ask students to call out other words to describe people's characters which begin with the letter 'G'. Make a list, adding words yourself if there are very obvious gaps in the students' knowledge, but taking care not to monopolise.
4 Do the same with seven or cight other letters.
5 When the lists are complete check all the words have been understood.
6 Then rub out the vocabulary and leave only the first letters.
7 Now ask the students to find a word beginning with one of these letters for the people in their family trees and to write the initial letter, not the word, next to each name.
8 When everyone's ready, pair the students, and have them sit side by side so they can look together at the diagram.
9 Ask them to take turns to present the members of their families, revealing the key character words for each and explaining why they chose them.

3.14

LANGUAGE FOCUS
Vocabulary to describe personal characteristics

LEVEL
Intermediate +

TIME
15–20 minutes

MATERIALS
Black/whiteboard, pen and paper

PREPARATION
None

3.15

LANGUAGE FOCUS
Oral practice

LEVEL
Intermediate +

TIME
20 minutes

MATERIALS
None

PREPARATION
None

COLOUR, SOUND, TASTE AND SMELL

This is a way to set up an intimate conversation in pairs. It's a good activity to use when the group is tired or needs a break from the here and now of intensive study.

Procedure

1 Ask the students to do the following preliminaries:
   a Clear the desks of books, pens, papers and bags.
   b Find a comfortable position in their chairs.
   c Relax (close their eyes if this helps).
   d Listen to your voice.
2 Invite them to think back to a place which has been important to them in the past and concentrate on it for a few moments. Allow a pause.
3 Then ask the students to remember a colour, a sound, a taste and a smell associated with that place. Allow another pause
4 Then have them sit face to face in pairs and talk to each other about the special place and the sensations it conjures up for them.
5 To finish, do a round in which each person in turn describes the one colour, sound, taste or smell, which the activity has brought to mind most strongly.

NOTES

Changing Energies (Agosta 1988) is a whole person TEFL activities book which gives lots of ideas for relaxation techniques with which to introduce this kind of conversation.

3.16

LANGUAGE FOCUS
Vocabulary expansion: everyday routines, oral practice

LEVEL
Intermediate +

TIME
15–20 minutes

MATERIALS
Pen and paper

PERSONAL ROUTINES

A conversation in which students work on the vocabulary they need to describe the minute details of their everyday routines. The activity shows how personal information of no particular significance in its own right becomes interesting when compared in a group.

PREPARATION

Observe the way you clean your teeth at night. Prepare a mime which includes all the details of your personal teeth-cleaning routine. Try not to leave anything out.

Procedure

1 Present your mime and ask the class to count the number of actions you make from start to finish.
2 Collect the students' observations. Ask them to notice how what we

generally think of as one event, such as cleaning teeth, is in fact a chain of actions. These actions, which are part of our daily lives and become deeply rooted habits, differ from person to person.

3 Choose with the class an everyday event such as dressing, taking a bath, having a family meal or going to bed, to work on for the rest of the lesson. Ask students to think of their own personal routine for these events.

4 Form groups of four or five in which the members compare their routines. The objective is for each member to find four differences between their way of doing things and that of the others. Circulate and supply new vocabulary as needed.

5 At the end of the group work, put all the new language on the board and ask the students to report back on their findings, using this vocabulary.

VARIATIONS

To make the comparison of routines visual (and to help get over possible shortages of vocabulary) ask students to mime their routines to each other in the sub-groups.

LOANS

In the first part of this activity students do a short values clarification. This is then linked to a specific language teaching point, that of making 'easy' and 'difficult' requests. Values clarification activities can give the teaching of communicative functions an element of psychological reality by creating an opening for the presentation and practice of new language related to things students feel and believe.

Procedure

1 Ask the students to divide a page of exercise paper into three columns and give them the following headings:

Easily, to anyone	Only to people I'm close to	Almost never

2 Briefly introduce the theme of lending and borrowing.

3 Ask the students to list in the first column their own personal possessions, including money, which they would be happy to lend to anyone, without giving it a second thought. In the second column

3.17

LANGUAGE FOCUS
Making requests with varying degrees of deference, oral practice

LEVEL
Intermediate

TIME
20–30 minutes

MATERIALS
Pen and paper

PREPARATION
None

they should write down things they own which they would only consider lending to a close friend or member of their family. In the third column they list possessions they are extremely reluctant to lend to anybody.

4 Pair the students and have them sit face to face. Tell them to exchange lists.

5 One student must choose an item from any of the columns on the partner's page and ask to borrow it, the other must respond according to the value they attach to the object. The situation is repeated three times, with a request for a different item each time.

6 Stop the activity and review the language the students have been using. The concept of easy and difficult requests should be clear; at this point, introduce the new language you think is most appropriate to the needs and level of your class. For example you might want to teach formula phrases such as:
Lend me your pen, will you?
Marco, would you mind awfully if I borrowed . . .
I'm terribly sorry to have to ask you this, but . . .
I wonder if you could possibly lend me . . .

7 Now ask students to swap roles and do the same activity again, this time using the new language.

8 Finish with a whole group discussion about why some things are less lendable than others and compare the different answers the students gave to the first task.

3.18

LANGUAGE FOCUS
can/can't + infinitive, oral practice

LEVEL
Elementary +

TIME
15–20 minutes

MATERIALS
Pen and paper

PREPARATION
None

JOHARI WINDOWS

An activity for conversation in pairs about aptitudes and accomplishments, topics which reveal interesting and surprising facts about people in a group and help bring it together.

Procedure

1 Ask students to pair with someone they would like to know better. One person in each pair will be 'A', the other 'B'.

2 Ask them to make a Johari Window, as in Fig. 11, and then to work together to complete it in the following way. In the top left hand box of the diagram they should write four things they can both do well, in the top right, four things 'A' can do but 'B' can't, in the bottom left four things that 'B' can do but 'A' can't and in the final box four things that neither of them can do well.

3 Finish with a round of *I was surprised to learn that . . .* (see Activity 3.3).

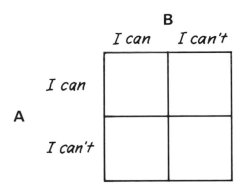

Fig. 11

VARIATIONS

Other Johari Window conversations can be based on the sentence beginnings *I like/don't like, I am/am not, I have/have never.*

DISCUSSION TICKETS

A discussion technique which guarantees equal participation from all the members of a group and can be used specifically to sensitise learners to problems of the dynamic of discussions in class. It's not practical for large groups.

Procedure

1 This activity works best if you can arrange the class in a circle or horseshoe so everybody can see everybody else.
2 Get each student to tear a page of exercise paper into four pieces and write on each piece 'Valid for one contribution'. Do the same yourself.
3 Explain that you will ask the group to discuss a topic of their choice and that every time someone speaks they must pay one ticket. Tickets are 'paid' by laying them on the floor in front of the speaker so they are visible to all. Every utterance, even a single word, must be paid for. The discussion will continue until all the tickets have been used up. Once you have spent your tickets you must sit back and listen – you can't intervene again. You aren't allowed to give your tickets away. (NOTE: The teacher has four tickets too and must abide by the rules like everybody else. This is important for the democracy of the activity.)
4 When the instructions are clear to the group, the discussion begins with the search for a topic to talk about. Be very firm about the rules from the outset, using gestures if you don't want to spend all your tickets at once!
5 At the end of the conversation, do a round of *In this lesson I have learned that . . .* (see Activity 3.3).

3.19

LANGUAGE FOCUS
Discussion

LEVEL
Intermediate +

TIME
15–20 minutes

MATERIALS
Exercise paper

PREPARATION
None

NOTES

We have learned a lot about the structure of discussions through doing this activity.

3.20

LANGUAGE FOCUS
Discussion

LEVEL
Intermediate +

TIME
10 minutes

MATERIALS
Token microphone

THE MICROPHONE

Another technique, similar to Activity 3.19, which helps train students in regulating their discussions by themselves.

PREPARATION

When you plan to hold a discussion with the whole class, bring into the lesson something that will represent a microphone (not a real microphone), for example, a piece of cardboard tube.

Procedure

1 Before you begin the discussion, explain the procedure the students are going to follow, holding the 'microphone' up in front of you as you speak. The rules are:
   - Whoever has the 'microphone' has the right to speak for as long as they want, and the others must listen in silence – no interruptions, no asides.
   - When the speaker has finished, they put down the 'microphone'. The next person who wants to speak raises a hand and the previous speaker gives them the piece of tube.
2 Let the discussion go on as long as interest is maintained. As in Activity 3.19 it is important that the teacher observes the same rules as the students. Once you have explained the rules you hand over the microphone, thus temporarily giving up your role as classroom manager. The group (of which, for the duration of the activity, you are a member and not the leader) organises the discussion by itself.

Bibliography

Agosta, J 1988 *Changing Energies* Pilgrims Publications

Brandes, D 1982, 1987 *Gamester's Handbook* Vol. 1 and 2 Hutchinson

British Council, The 1978 *Communication Games* (Video)

Frank, C, Rinvolucri, M and Berer, M 1982 *Challenge to Think* Oxford University Press

Maley, A and Duff, A 1982 *Drama Techniques in Language Learning* New Edition Cambridge University Press

Morgan, J and Rinvolucri, M 1984 *Once Upon a Time* Cambridge University Press

Morgan, J and Rinvolucri, M 1986 *Vocabulary* Oxford University Press

Moskowitz, G 1978 *Caring and Sharing in the Foreign Language Classroom* Newbury House

Rinvolucri, M 1984 *Grammar Games* Cambridge University Press

Stevick, E 1980 *Teaching Languages: A Way and Ways* Newbury House

Wagner, B. 1979 *Dorothy Heathcote: Drama as a Learning Medium* Heinemann